REFLECTIONS

Selected Poems by

Jim Reiman

Contents

THE GREEN GATE 5

CREATION'S SONG 6

REQUIEM 7

BLACK BEAR 8

CHICKADEE 10

BROOK TROUT 11

JUDGEMENT DAY 12

TWENTY-TWENTY 13

THE WORLD ON FIRE 14

BUDDA AND THE JAY 16

SEED AND LEAF 17

WATCHING TIME 18

ATWOOD BROOK 19

I WALKED TO THE RIVER TO FISH 20

I LIVE HERE 22

THE PLOWMAN AND THE STORM 23

WATCHING AT DAWN 25

I AM OLD NOW 26

HAIKU CALENDAR 27

THE FISHERMAN 29

PACAYA 30

THE DEATH OF MY FATHER 30

BLIND FAITH 31

INTERSECTION 33

KEEPING TRACK OF LOVE 35

SO GO AHEAD 36

WHAT MATTERS 38

LOCOMOTIVE 40

BEULAH 42

MY STREET 44

BUDDY 45

AT SIXTY 47

FOR BUDDY 47

DREAMING OF THE HUNT 49

MORNING IN MEMPHIS 53

SAN PEDRO 54

MACAU 57

A NIGHT IN SAIGON 58

SON LOI 59

TOI XIN LOI (I'M SORRY) 59

MAROSTICA 62

THE GREEN GATE

the green gate hangs crooked on one hinge
attached at the shoulder with an iron ring
to a standing stone post

the gate is open and tilts slightly
a sweeping arm gesturing
to enter rather than keep out

a short way beyond the gate
a small sign says
stay on the path

a message
perhaps
words of wisdom
to help you find your way

though it's only a furrow of foot trampled ground
twisting upwards
it will take you to where you want to go

and once there
you'll know where you've come from
and beyond

CREATION'S SONG

I heard a sound the other day
it came from some place far way
the sound of notes so sweetly played
on strings
from a harp that god has made
is it the sound of time begun
that perfect note of only one
that one clear perfect note I heard
joined by other notes until
the notes swirl and dance in perfect form
and soon a perfect song is born
a song so sweet night turns to day
the void of darkness is swept away
and on and on the notes will play
in rhythm of the cosmos sway
from empty space that song is sung
creation's bells of birth are rung
the nothingness that was before
now creation's song forevermore
until eternity no longer sings
until the bells no longer ring
until the light of day is gone
and notes no longer make that song

REQUIEM

On learning of the death of three billion song birds

a wind whispered song
accompanied by dawn
a refrain we strain to hear

silent now for a moment
and then again
just the faint flutter of wings

and a few notes
crystal chimes
from high above

a line or two
from a melody of a life
that used to be and is no more

BLACK BEAR

In the early spring
on the back side of Chateauguay near my home
the bears come out hungry from under the winter snow

in the fading afternoon light I followed fresh tracks
over the frozen brook
to a small opening between two trees

and there something dark and still
paused and faced me
at the edge of the woods

share your dreams with me I asked
with my eyes
and his eyes answered

magic exists
between us
he inhaled my fear

in eerie silence the conversation continued
I could smell him
and he me

fear is necessary his eyes said
it is what holds us in this moment
feel it and understand it's power

in those seconds of stillness
I felt strangely safe
under the spell of his presence

then silently as the last bit of dim light came between us
he drew his blackness around him like a cloak
and turned to the woods and the darkness

stepping into the magic of night
he slowly he slipped into the shadow of spruce and hemlock
and disappeared taking with him so much that is still unknown

CHICKADEE

I hold the silver and the black body
in my hand
a cradled warm nest
the tiny black eyes open and close
reflecting the world beyond me
a prefect triangle beak
opens and closes
clasping for air
rising and falling
waves of air
in the rhythm of the flight
interrupted by a piece of glass
an illusion
broken
along with the tiny bones
that holds all life together
briefly
until the head droops
and the breath ebbs
as life's spirit lifts
and continues the flight
back through the glass
into the crystal sky
at once and everywhere

BROOK TROUT

This morning on the edge of a spring stream
mist soft as warm breath against the cold

below the glassy film
quick shadows crisscross sun drenched pebbles

smooth mahogany darts – speckled with red dots
skitter under alder boughs

I stood to watch them settle
at the edge of the eddy

arranged in a phalanx
steadied there with a modest sway of a fin

an asterisk of an insect
drifts in the crease of the current

swiftly …rising on sun sparkling water
the first in line lifts it's bullet-like head

the smooth tea colored water dimples
and the surface is sipped clean

JUDGEMENT DAY

before the snow goes
before the crocuses see the sun
clusters of Red-Winged Blackbirds
perch on cattails and birch boughs

above the marsh pond
they cackle like supreme judges
in their glossy black robes
with sashes of red and yellow

complaining
under an ominous sky
in a cacophonous choir
they weigh the evidence

nature will have it's way
is the verdict
then as a cold dark wind descends
they scatter and are gone

leaving us alone
impotent in our dying world
with only our fear
and our helplessness

TWENTY-TWENTY

twenty-twenty
fell hard
on people everywhere

billions of eyes blinked open each day
everyone sees the same cracks
widening in the sky

not just
darkness creeping
between the cracks of light

but the ominous sound
the heavenly clutch
shift

trying to hold the heavy load
racing head long
down the steep cold slope

where only prayers
behind blinking eyes
will save us

THE WORLD ON FIRE

We are at the edge of the burning land
flames at our backs
blue green sea stretches before us

angry angels rise with wings afire
hovering above the waves
steaming death over the dead coral

the horror is real
but it's also an abstract image for all to see from afar
beamed across oceans on TV

we sit dumb at home to the horror
we sit dumb waiting in airports to the horror
necks crooked upward to the monitor

looking at the blood red fires of the apocalypse
and the face of a cuddly little bear singed
by the flames

just like the little bear
you snuggled with
when you were innocent and cried for comfort

let me say now
there is no innocence
little child no comfort

the monster has escaped
and it lives among us every day
and here we are now

trying to learn about the monster
and the horror
but there's a commercial break

it's all about prescriptions
for everything that ales you
with endless disclaimers

about how the cure might kill you
but you need the cure anyway
desperately

because your nerves are busting through your skin
and you really don't feel so good lately
so pay attention and get this stuff

they'll tell you how to order it
now back to live TV
back to the horror

and the apocalypse
and when you've had too much of all of this
just push the button

BUDDA AND THE JAY

At the peak of the storm
the jay is perched on the head of Buddha
near the corner of the garden

where dry stems of weathered phlox rattle in the wind
coal black eyes penetrate the blinding blizzard
contemplating this precise moment

the shape of every exquisite flake of snow that is falling
fixed in this moment
frozen and motionless

in the driving snow
against the wind
and the whiteness

lost in the sky
the jay disappears into
a blue grey cloud

Seed and Leaf

For forty years I've walked this land
and seen the seasons change
and days pile on one another
like fallen leaves layer the moist earth
and each new fallen leaf a crumbled page
with a story of its own

and while the memory of its time
slowly fades and decays
it nourishes the waiting seed below
until the sun and warm spring rain
give life to sprouts that soon are tendrils green
and so begins the cycle of life again

WATCHING TIME

I watched snow
deep in the woods
in mid winter
in perfect silence

large flakes floating
 seconds then minutes
piling on one another
fragile chips of time

I stood transfixed for a full hour
the accumulation of an inch
between the trees
silver gray

parachuting particles
remembered
more as moments
than snow

ATWOOD BROOK

I stand here on my land
and think back to my time
next to the brook
where I built my cabin
three summers there
I drank the water
and washed
and slept deeply
to the notes of night music
water swirling pools
dancing dark cold
threads of water
twisting through rocks
and moss-covered deadfalls
flecks of moonlight
beam back
light and music
I awake under its spell
and hear a voice speak to me
in water words
that release me
from my the earthly bond
as my mind flows
and water whispers
magical words
first just babble
then a prayer loud and clear
I strain to hear

I WALKED TO THE RIVER TO FISH

I walked to the river to fish
but there was no water
I walked across gray flat stones
where runs of trout would skitter to safety
along the deep cut banks
but they were gone now
maybe a few
on the bottom
in pocket pools of cool water
waiting for rain
that wasn't coming
not today anyway
I knew it would be like this
but I came to see
not fish
and sit at the river's edge
and remember my childhood
when I would come here
and catch as many as I wanted
and please my mom
when she would fry them for dinner
and say to me I could go fishing anytime
as far as she was concerned
because she loved fried trout
pink and sweet
like salmon
with butter and lemon
delicious
sweet memories

of the easy flowing river
and speckled native trout
and my smiling mom

I LIVE HERE

I live here on this piece of ground
where spruce trees twice my age
grew in abundance
in the dark moist soil by the brook

I cut them down
and stripped their bark

chiseled and spiked
they have become the bones of my house
the skeleton of
rafters joists and beams

I know them
from fifty years ago

nicks and notches here and there
the slip of my saw
today they are
imperfect reminders
of so many years
by the brook
on this piece of earth
surrounded by trees
I have come to know so well

THE PLOWMAN AND THE STORM

the storm rages in the mountains above the house
I wait for the plowman
in the dark morning hours

between four and five
lying awake waiting
straining to hear

through the wind and snow and darkness
far below
but above the rattling wind chimes

I hear the sound of the distant machine straining
up the hill a half mile away
as the plowman nears the top

the engine screams pushing hard
the plow busts through waves of foamy snow
a ship headlong into the gale

daring not to slow
stopping is not an option
rumbling past my window with yellow lights flashing

slipping further into the storm
the lights dim
the roar of the engine melts into the darkness

at the top of road
deep in the woods the wind is furious
he stops and backs to turn around

before the downhill run
in the warm cab bathed in yellow dashboard lights
he sits and opens his thermos

this is a good place to take a break
I know it well
the end of the road

spruce trees surround the place holding back the driving snow
the little brook runs free along the road
even on the coldest days

near the plowman's truck
a stone wall lies
buried beneath the snow

I made a seat of flat stones
many years ago
to sit and rest on frequent walks

now I think of him there
as he sips his coffee
gazing into driving snow

down the hill I listen to the wind

WATCHING AT DAWN

still dark
I watched the dawn come on
rose on snow
finches come
 in clouds of yellow gray
and dance a funny dance
to dust the snow away
and gather round
singing
giving thanks
for another day

I AM OLD NOW

I am old now
but not stiff
like most old things

a beautiful young woman
with an old soul
has adopted me

she feeds me
potions from flowers
that grow wild in her field

in kindness we share
the blessings of old ways
and the magic of healing

haiku calendar

JANUARY
snow deep as cold holds
the earth below in silence
suspended in time

FEBRUARY
sun frozen crystals
dividing the fractured light
red yellow green blue

MARCH
the mountain and sky
embracing the fading light
one star shining bright

APRIL
blue mist drifts over
the diamond rippling water
speckled trout below

MAY
the pebble drifted
slowly in crystal water
catching day's last light

JUNE
a raven circled
above the towering spruce
silently watching

JULY
blue green dragon fly
 summer heat and golden sky
here now then goodbye

AUGUST
corn tassels dancing
swaying masts of verdant green
shadows arching down

SEPTEMBER
the painted ladies
are in abundance feeding
on flowering mint

OCTOBER
a gold leaf tinged red
floats free on the still water
life and death at once

NOVEMBER
the black bear turns and
disappears into shadows
of eternal night

DECEMBER
Yuletide candlelight
distant cabin window bright
cold moon floating snow

The Fisherman

He walks silently to the ocean
down the steep steps into the valley
on the jungle path of moss and brick red clay
deeply descending through hau
and cat's paw and hala
to the semi circle reef
that embraces the surf and calms it
to the emerald pool that quivers with life
he swings his net
to the rhythm of the waves
copper colored shoulders
broad and strong
cast to tidal pools of jade and silver
deep blue below
the arching net
the ocean's treasures gathered
the rainbow fish are dancing
the man and fish are one

Kauai

PACAYA

THE DEATH OF MY FATHER

on that clear morning
at the beginning of the millennium
pacaya spoke for my father
his final breath erupting in thick black clouds
rushing towards heaven howling
I have loved you my son

later that day
pure white and brilliant
on the black beach of monte rico
just after I wrote a love song
a scorpion placed a tiny dagger of death in my back
betraying the peaceful lyrics of words so sweet

that night dark and silent
beneath a thatched roof
I dreamed a terrible dream
my heart beat to the thundering rhythm
of the pacific surf
my scream shattered the black night

darkness descended
I felt the blood of my father
drain from my body
I awoke
abandoned and alone
fatherless in another world

BLIND FAITH

Believe this and you will find the truth…
"who said that ?"
I asked the seer

He said, "I did…
and that's that !"
then to myself I whispered a prayer

for wisdom I prayed
to help guide my thoughts
through the amazing world I live in

searching and seeking in silence
to know
the origin of original sin

deep troubled waters I crossed
strange mysteries to ponder
saints singing God's sacred songs

I now stand before them
and shout it out loud
"I've done nothing" and nothing is wrong

but Augustine in his moment of torment
withered mind and wandering
about the garden that day

thought how could they say no
how could they refuse
one small bite of life so sweet

then paradise was lost forever
and now I with ugly serpent skin stand lost and confused
for I too crave such sweetness

it wasn't God's wish that day
I said to Old Saint A
that doomed so many souls for so long

INTERSECTION

they saw the light at that exact moment
brilliant April sun… just up
windows cracked….a bit
streaming cool sweet spring air

ahead
the colors clicked
green yellow red
STOP

through windshields
gray with winter smudge
across the empty intersection
face to face now

between them across the black asphalt
wet with dew
thirty years of separation
stretch before them…heavy and broken

she stares at him disbelieving
a ray of sun shoots over her head like a finger pointing
it lights up his face
it is so much softer now she thinks…perhaps even sad

love once reigned
young love
so powerful so tender
they never knew what they had

the light changes
a green arrow points
but, he's a gentle man and waits
and she passes by him once again

from the side
she's radiant
he goes straight on
towards the sun

KEEPING TRACK OF LOVE

you can't measure love in days or months
years or hours

love doesn't bother with time
rather it flows like water

sometimes slow and deep
other times fast and wild

but always onward
gaining strength along the way

love's course cannot be charted
only love knows where it's going

and being in love is a journey
to places unknown

ever changing
yet trusting it's direction

we look back now
over the years

and know well
we two are

like water
flowing to the sea

SO GO AHEAD

So go ahead and follow the twisted route of thought
down the road of the so-called intellectuals
coming back to think it over again
gape mouthed and dumb to it all
so much so it that brings you to a place so far beyond compre-
hension
you circle back and ask yourself about that old girlfriend
and wonder what ever happened to her
while some smart ass doctor tells you
it had to do with something deep inside your consciousness
and you never realized you didn't have a chance of getting her in
the first place
and later on in psych one-o-one you think you hear him again
once again trying to explain it
so you listen not so intently
instead you're looking back ten rows
and seeing that dream girl of your lifetime
and know to meet her would solve all of your problems
because of the bob of her ginger colored hair
and her smart round tortoise shell glasses
and the soft smoothness of her slender neck
and the beige cashmere sweater
too big for her to be wearing in the first place
he's still trying to explain exactly what happened back then
when all you wanted was someone
who wanted you
to hold them close
and feel the warmth of that sweater
and pull her towards you

and know that she wanted you to kiss her deeply
and love you for what you hope you could be for her
in the next minute or hour
or lifetime

WHAT MATTERS

for me
report card time
in fifth grade
was frightening

K through four didn't matter
but the fifth did

it was always the same
I could do better
that was the bottom line
I wasn't applying myself
not working to my full potential
I didn't pay attention

I was ten
I didn't know what it meant
potential
I studied frogs and turtles and snakes
and potentially I was the smartest kid
if you wanted to know about frogs and turtles and snakes
and where you could find them

but not my teacher Miss V
she didn't hear me
she said I talked too much
and she didn't like frogs and turtles and snakes
or the mud flats
or the raft I built by the creek

now I see that potential doesn't matter
what matters is doing what matters to you
and as far as paying attention
I paid attention
to things that matter most …as it turns out
like frogs and turtles and snakes

Locomotive

I conjure every detail of the day
my father
took me to see the locomotive
in the shop as big as a baseball stadium
where he worked
on the New York New Haven and Hartford

hundreds of mercury vapor lights
on the ceiling
lit up the big black machine

greasy clouds of welding smoke
filled the air with the stench of ozone
smells suspended in a gauzy film
closed in

the iron beast hovered over me with an evil presence
dark and menacing
one big eye staring at me

my father climbed the ladder
into the cab
towering over me
he yelled down
wanna hear me start her up

below
small timid fearful
I screamed
no

he climbed down
gently took my trembling hand
we went home
he was quiet all the way

BEULAH

when I was in grade school my mother would take us on the bus
buying back-to-school clothes
at the end of summer
in the department store downtown

I saw a black person for the first time
sitting across from me
she was big with a bright red napkin tied to her head
and too many bags at her feet

loudly I said to my mother
that's Beulah from television
shut up
my mother hissed

then Beulah took me in with her dark eyes
to know me better
smiling eyes full of love
I looked at her wishing to say something

don't stare
my mother hissed again
why
she looks nice I whispered back

downtown the bus emptied at Shartenbergs where we would
shop
all except Beulah

her eyes followed me off the bus
she smiled right at me again

I watched her in the window as the bus pulled away
she opened her hand
five long fingers and a pink and white palm
back and forth her hand waved until the bus was gone

later in the store I asked my mother
where's Beulah going
to the end of the line
she said

MY STREET

my street
elm shrouded in my boyhood days
like a tunnel
a stadium of sorts
I tossed long looping spirals from pole to pole
for touchdowns on the hot asphalt
you watched me
from your window up above
and smiled at our little boy games
but later on
on the salt flats
you and I explored
the crazy maze of cat tails
we swam naked across the green creek
clothes held high above our heads
you were so cool
your summer skin so smooth
you sparkled with water beads
we dried ourselves in the sun
and whispered because we were afraid of being together like this
knotted like serpents
so tightly in the moment
I so close to your neck
and the smell of your wet hair
and the warm grass
you said I was your hero
as I saw past you
to the whitecaps racing across the harbor

Buddy

I was a teenager in love
in the winter of fifty-nine
when I got home from school that day
Jimmy C came down to the basement

where we listened to a standup Magnavox
with the enormous dial that glowed amber
this is what we did where I lived
back when rock and roll was born

and Jimmy didn't have to tell me what happened
because Allen Freed was playin' one right after the other on
WINS
that's why he came down after school
so we sat and listened

words of love
whispered soft and true
hold me close and tell me how you feel
tell me love is real

I held Peggy Sue in my hand
 a 45 Coral yellowish orange
everyday was the flip side
everyday seems a little longer everyway love's a little stronger

I wanted so much to be with my girl right then
she would need me to hold her tight

cause
I'm gonna need my baby tonight

in the background between songs
there was talk
a small plane
a snowy field

but the fact is
me and jimmy just couldn't take it all in
it was too much back then
when we were teenagers

and there were so many possibilities
but now fifty years later my heart is wide open
and it feels good to be quiet and listen again to that music
and remember the day it fell from the sky

AT SIXTY

FOR BUDDY

for so many years
I have marked the day
and close my eyes to see
the faded photo
black and white
the cornfield
strewn with rubble
and broken stalks
it mystifies the eye
that long dark rutted harrow
the road to eternity
gouged in the snow

I pause
a sweet refrain rises
and I strain
to listen
torn between
sound and sight
the tormented image
the echoing refrain
growing and flowing
across the field
out to the dawn horizon
echoing across the plain
across the country
around the world

a melody
a beat
on and on
shuffling
in time
a slap
a clap
the snap of fingers
the strain of strings
a voice
so sweet
it will never die

DREAMING OF THE HUNT

I was a man-boy long before the dawn
when I left my bed
and remember only that I was dreaming wide awake
in the morning darkness
silver shapes from moon and stars
shined through panes of old cracked window glass
crusted heavy with hoary frost
casting spider-web patterns of light on the bare bedroom floor
and in the kitchen
the sweet scent of an all night log
consumed but for its ember form
lingered in the parlor stove
along with remnant smells of last night's dinner
in an old cast iron pan atop the blackened stove
barely glowing rosy now
little heat and quiet within
I took the chair there
and lit the lamp
and sat before a pile of woolen clothes
pants socks shirt vest jacket gloves cap
I stretched a thick sock on to each foot
and tugged the wooly plaids over well-worn cotton johns
wrestling with myself in the near dark room
into these clothes for cold
and to the stove I added a singled splintered chunk of seasoned
ash
atop the dying coals
it flared
and soon the snaps and pops of crackling wood

kindled in time and made the kitchen warm
while coffee perked in its enamel pot of blue
and bacon sizzled side by side the slabs of thick dark bread
I ate the toast and bacon with black coffee
and sat quietly by the stove in the coming light
but in this midst
while still in the stupor of my sleep and dreams
which hung heavy in the moment
my mind traced tracks of yesterday
to the place on the pinnacle of spruce and pines
where the big buck slept
dark and distant
in sleep and dreaming
my thoughts rose above me
as I made my way past barns and fields
and found in the dark dawn the old log road
towards the distant peak
now a silhouette against the gun gray sky
out there as it has been long before my dream or dreams of
others
iron-hard granite gray shapes stood steep above the snowy earth
so slowly I went
cold beneath my boots
and jagged shards of pine above
I knew this beast from other days
once from far across a frozen fen
I watched as he lowered his muscled neck
to drink deeply from a winter spring
the rack he wore was massive and mighty
and his cape was dark as gray can be
this old buck strong in his knowledge of these woods
sensed distant dangers
and felt my presence from his safe place

and yet the heavy slumber could not be shaken
from my head
and made me wonder if I was truly here
or somehow in another world unknown to men
yet known to those who dwelled among these trees
these hills so steep and valleys deep
stepping through soft snow
no sound I brought along with me
I knew the sleeping buck would hear
the slightest snap of twigs or leaves
that broke or rattled from a tree
I do not know what made me stop
just below the mountain peak
my dream held me in this place
below the crest and cold slate sky
but there I stood and waited for the changing light
to show me to the place the buck might be
bedded in a glen of mossy rocks and spruce
just one way in
but not for my eyes to see
the dream then took my mind beyond
my thoughts now turned to something else
senses sharpened to a razor's edge
lifting me from where I stood to a place I feared to be
for now before me I could see the beast at rest
bedded down and unaware of me
but in a flash the purpose of my presence there broke through
and I in that instant sensed the scent of death descend
upon both man and beast
as two hearts soared together in the mossy glen
for it was death I dreamed
to take me to this place and in this moment
when I looked into his frozen eye

my finger on the trigger eased
he stood
still for just an instant
and turned and walked away from me

MORNING IN MEMPHIS

one endless night we played old forty fives
until the Sun came up in Memphis
and another day stretched out flat and brilliant
lighting up everything on its journey

across wide rivers and slumbering mountains
past crystal cities under violet skies
it was all in the future
and we listened in silence

before I fell into a deep sleep I said
tonight we went so far back
I think we have found a home
together among these incredible notes

all of this is so new you said
it's Ok
I said
spin another
I think I'm really going to enjoy growing up with you

SAN PEDRO

In the cradle of the catskills
by a river in the warm spring sun
close by me
my youthful friends and I made a circle
and held hands with san pedro
the brother of mescalito from the desserts of the south
to embark on an epic journey
down a river to places unimagined

our boat of brilliant smooth wood
polished clean on the green water
and gleaming sails of pure white
filled with cool cobalt air
took us from our safe sandy shores to an island
crowned with low slung dreamy clouds
and soaring mountains green and lush
with succulent fruit and ginger scented grass

that night on bare ground
with ears to the warm spring soil
we heard the voice of san pedro call us to duty
so as to continue our voyage to fantastic things
our eyes beheld each other and we laughed at our contorted
selves
and screamed at the intruders we thought would not let us
escape
from the visions we sought to rend to dust
and rid our fear of the rising waters

our vessel rocked in the blue green foam
in waves of fabric fashioned from long forgotten looms
that wrapped around us and held us to our course
across ripples of diamond studded currents
under collapsing skies streaked with red and gold and ribbons of
violet

then our captain
the fearless san pedro
came upon the deck
slick with tears from laughter and rage
he said
boys I'm afraid we've lost our way
but steady lads and know now for certain
our compass must be abandoned

even as the storm clouds thicken
and the waters become more treacherous
we must navigate with blinded eyes

we clung to the shear walls of the deck
holding hands crying and choking at our folly
at the insane storm thundering in our brains
grinning like fearless madmen
powerless but determined to find our way
to the heart of our fear
to come to grips with deliverance
and find the depth of the unknown night filled with terror

howling and hideous with monstrous visions
that pressed down on us with the weight of the deepest ocean
until we surrendered to our childlike weakness
and fell upon the deck in utter exhaustion

in the morning a sliver of silver sun pierced the blackness
and pointed towards a tiny strip on the broken horizon
an island floating in the wreckage of the storm
we set our course and bowed to the rising sun
cloud angels came down with golden bowls of cool spring water
and our dry mouths sucked deeply
as if life itself depended on satisfying our thirst

soon san pedro dropped from view into the pure blue water
below without a word
abandon and alone
one by one we followed but he was gone
the island was warm and clean and there was not a whisper of
wind nor sound
we gathered sticks of copper colored drift wood and sparked a
fire with flint
soon the smoke began to sing as it encircled us and twisted
upward to the cosmos
as if spun from colors unknown
we felt it's smooth touch and coolness as it embraced us as one
and effortlessly lifted us skyward to our journey's end

MACAU

The haze of distant fires lay thick
on the water of the South China Sea
slick and foul with sludge
gurgling thick and black
beneath our battered bow
I saw in the empty face of our helmsman
no recollection of how it was
or could ever be again
squinting through crinkled skin
his piercing dark eyes denying old memories
of the temples of the dead
the sweet smell of incense
as the blood red sun
goes down for the last time
along with his dreams of long forgotten traders
and visions of white lugsails
sturdy and square
cutting through waves
laden rich with spices
heavy in the water
against the wind

A NIGHT IN SAIGON

Silk shrouded girls
pale blue and white
glide through the thick night
like statues sculpted by the wind

they cross the wide boulevard
darting through the rush of rumbling motorbikes
and the tide of noisy metal crashing
through flickering glittering neon

storm clouds ascend suddenly
through the mist and fumes
and in the panic and swirl and noise
you stop

their grace and beauty beckons you to look back
and consider the exquisite contrast
between splendor and ruin
then the sound of a single night bird sings above the din

one single note
so sweet and gentle
it wraps around you
like an orchid petal

SON LOI

TOI XIN LOI (I'm sorry)

in an hour near dawn
we make our way to the river
to our long dugout canoe
soon we are pushing hard against the ebbing tide of the mekong
from our bow gentle waves are left behind
a sparkling V in the early morning sun
the rhythm of the wake
bends the slender stalks of grass along the shore
vivid visions flash before me of another time
the scabs of war have peeled off
and fallen away
but scars remain
along the banks
hollow craters
pock the land
strangely beautiful
sculpted by bombs
forms now lush with jungle grass
hide the lies of what happened here
hours up the river
snaking our way beneath bent mangroves
the sun full up
dappled light splinters through the rich green ceiling above
our boat slips silently on to a small beach
a long finger like island
at the sharp bend in the river
there a gray temple leans into the muddy earth

where stone priests and snarling dragons have toppled to the
ground
and are now half buried in a nest of clay and shiny vines
we take pictures
our guide speaks to us in a sing-song of sweet notes
and tells us of this ancient holy place
but she is too young and too pretty
to translate the ugly truth
I asked her silently
tell me of you mother
and your father
tell me of your brothers
and your sisters
tell me of your aunts and uncles
and their children
tell me about the dead
tell me about the crippled and maimed
tell me about everything that was lost forever
she lowers her head
her hands clasped in front
silently with deep brown sad eyes
she shows us a place in the shade
where we sit on hand-chiseled stone steps
we have lunch
served from large weed-woven baskets
covered with pretty cloth
we eat small rice cakes
with sweet and sour shrimp
and mint tea
her long thin fingers wrap brightly colored bits of vegetables in
lettuce leaves
she bows her head and serves each of us with a faint smile
we dip the lettuce rolls into a small bowl of tangy sauce

my heart is aching
but her grace is a prayer of forgiveness
yet before I go I want to say something
I wait until our eyes meet
and in a whisper I say
the only words of her language I have memorized
toi xin loi
son loi
I am sorry

MAROSTICA

Italy in late march
or early april
is best
like I remember it
years ago
even the songbirds know it's the time of year
to hang their little tidbits of music
in the budding trees pale green
inspired by the light I think
in early spring
to sing so sweetly
those impossible notes
suspended like ornaments in the air
which then rain down to the table below
drops of sweet music
gently falling on you
and your secret lover
into your bowl of zuppa
with white beans and pasta
and a bit of crusty bread